What is a slash used for in poetry?

What are some common uses of the comma?

Describe a comma splice.

Describe a sentence fragment.

Describe an appositive.

What are some common uses of the semicolon?

1. Commas may be used to separate the items in a sequence (three or more things). For example, "She went to the store, dropped off the clothes at the dry cleaners, and stopped by the post office."

2. Use a comma along with a conjunction (and, but, for, nor, yet, or, so) to connect two independent clauses. For example, "She wanted to go to the store, but she did not have a car."

3. Use a comma to set off introductory elements. For example, "Driving to the grocery store, she suddenly realized that she forgot her purse."

4. Use a comma to set off parenthetical elements. For example, "The Statue of Liberty, which stands in New York Harbor, was a gift to the United States."

A slash (/) is used to separate lines of poetry that are part of the text of a paper. An example would be this line of poetry: "What soft, cherubic creatures / these gentle women are / One would as soon assault a plush / or violate a star."

Sentence fragments happen by treating a dependent clause or other incomplete thought as a complete sentence. This error can typically be corrected by combining it with another sentence to make a complete thought.

Incorrect: Because I forgot the exam was today.
Correct: I forgot the exam was today.

A comma splice is the use of a comma between two independent clauses. A comma splice can typically be corrected by changing the comma to a period and therefore making the two clauses into two separate sentences, by changing the comma to a semicolon, or by making one clause dependent by inserting a dependent marker word in front of it.

Incorrect: She eats an apple every day, it tastes delicious.
Correct: She eats an apple every day. It tastes delicious.

(or) She eats an apple every day; it tastes delicious.

(or) She eats an apple every day, and it tastes delicious.

(or) She eats an apple every day because it tastes delicious.

(or) Because it tastes delicious, she eats an apple every day.

1. Semicolons are used to join independent clauses that aren't joined by a coordinating conjunction. For example, "Susie has brown hair; Susie's brother has red hair."

2. Semicolons are used to join two independent clauses connected by a conjunctive adverb or a transition word. For example, "In Washington D.C., she visited the National Archives; however, she never made it to the Smithsonian Institute."

3. Semicolons are used to separate items in a sequence containing internal punctuation. For example, "Our evening activities are first, cook dinner; second, eat dinner; third, exercise."

An appositive is a word or phrase that restates or modifies an immediately preceding noun. An appositive is often useful as a context clue for determining or refining the meaning of the word or words to which it refers. For example, "My dad, whose name is James Brown, (appositive) is a lawyer.

Provide examples of conjunctive adverbs and transition words.

Discuss apostrophe uses.

Describe colon uses.

How is a dash used?

What are some common uses of quotation marks?

What are the uses of an ellipsis?

1. Use an apostrophe for contractions. Example: has not – hasn't

2. Use an apostrophe to show possession with plural nouns ending in "s". Example: the boys' cars

Conjunctive adverbs include the following: also, besides, consequently, finally, furthermore, however, indeed, likewise, moreover, nevertheless, next, nonetheless, otherwise, similarly, specifically, then, therefore

Transition Words include the following: as a matter of fact, as a result, at the same time, for example, for instance, in addition, in conclusion, in fact, in the first place, on the other hand, to the contrary

Dashes are used (--) before an explanatory list following a complete sentence (A dash is less formal than a colon.) For example, "The coach gave her an exercise schedule--run three miles every other day, lift weights three times a week, stretch morning and evening, and swim laps.

The stew calls for all of the following--lamb, pork, tomatoes, and onions.

1. Use a colon before an explanatory list following a complete sentence. For example, "The boy had an interest in one of the following: softball, soccer, football, or basketball.

2. Use a colon before an independent clause that follows and explains the previous sentence.

3. Use a colon before a quotation.

4. Patrick Henry once said: "Give me liberty or give me death."

5. Use a colon after the greeting in a formal letter.
Dear Mr. President:
Dear Madam:

1. Use an ellipsis to indicate that you deleted words from a quotation.

2. Use an ellipsis to omit a sentence within a quotation, use an ellipsis and a period (....).

1. Use double quotation marks(" ") to enclose direct quotes. Example – Nathan Hale said, "I only regret that I have but one life to lose for my country."

2. Use double quotation marks to enclose titles of chapters of books, newspaper & magazine articles, short stories, songs and poems.

3. Use single quotation marks (' ') to set off a quotation within a quotation. Example - Dr. Sherman said that "George Washington did not say 'I cannot tell a lie' although Americans enjoy believing that he did."

Describe the function of an adjective.

Describe the differences between an independent clause and a dependent clause. Also discuss the various types of dependent clauses.

Discuss equal comparison adjectives.

Discuss unequal comparison adjectives.

Describe adjective phrases.

Describe the function of an adverb.

An *independent clause* is a group of words that contains a subject and verb and expresses a complete thought. An independent clause is a sentence.

A *dependent clause* is a group of words that contains a subject and verb but does not express a complete thought. A dependent clause cannot be a sentence. Dependent clauses can be a noun clause, adjective clause, or an adverb clause.

A *noun clause* can be a subject, a direct or indirect object, or an object of a preposition. Noun clauses can begin with wh- question words (what, which, when, where, who, whom) and question words like how, if, that.

An *adjective clause* modifies a noun or a pronoun. An adjective clause begins with who, whom, which, that, whose, when, where, why and follows the word it modifies.

An *adverb clause* modifies a verb, an adjective, another adverb, or a sentence. An adverb clause answers the question when? where? why? how? to what degree? and under what condition? An adverb clause begins with a subordinating conjunction, such as after, because, since, unless, etc.

Unequal comparisons:
Comparative: to compare two things use -er/more, less.
Superlative: to refer to the one in a group of three or more that is the outstanding example, use -est/most, least.

One-syllable adjectives use -er/est or less/least
Positive: new
Comparative: newer
Superlative: the newest

Two-syllable adjectives ending in 'y' use -er/est or less/least
Positive: hungry
Comparative: hungrier
Superlative: the hungriest

Two or more syllables use more/most; less/least
Positive: thrilling
Comparative: more thrilling
Superlative: the most thrilling

A few adjectives have irregular comparative and superlative forms.
Positive: bad
Comparative: worse than
Superlative: the worst

An *adverb* modifies a verb, an adjective, or another adverb by answering such questions as how? how much? how long? when? and where? Adverbs also act as sentence modifiers.
1. He dressed handsomely. how?
2. She knows more than she thinks. how much?
3. He was gone a week. how long?
3. Last month they flew to Hawaii. when?
4. I went home. where?
5. Unfortunately, he revealed the story's surprise ending. sentence modifier

Other Parts of Speech as Adverbs - Nouns, prepositions and adjectives sometimes act as adverbs.
1. I'll see you Friday. noun when?
2. He came outside. preposition where?
3. My brother Fred runs slow. adjective how?

Adverbs Formed by Adding 'LY' to Adjectives - An adverb is often formed by adding an 'ly' to an adjective.

An *adjective* modifies a noun, a pronoun, or another adjective by answering the following questions: What kind of? Which one? How many? How much?

Adjectives can appear in three places: before a noun, after a linking or sensory verb (be, feel, look, seem, smell, sound, etc.), and after a direct object as an objective complement.
Examples:
1. The United States is a wonderful place to live. (adjective is before a noun)
2. The baby seems happier after a nap. (adjective follows a linking verb)
3. The military has worked to keep us safe. (the adjective is an objective complement)

Nouns, pronouns, and participles sometimes act as adjectives.
Examples:
1. The student government elected a president. noun
2. This is a exciting time. present participle
3. We viewed the demolished building. past participle
4. This china is very old. demonstrative pronoun
5. Which movie did you see? interrogative pronoun
6. His haircut was hideous. possessive pronoun

Equal comparisons - Use as...as to compare two persons, places, or things which are apparently the same.
Examples:
1. He is as short as I am.
2. Her cat is as fussy as his cat is.
3. Josh's swing is as old and rusty as mine is.
4. That little chair is as expensive as my big sofa.

Adjective phrases are groups of words used as adjectives.

Participial phrases consist of a participle, its object, and any modifiers. Participles show tense and voice.
1. The boy shooting the ball is the team captain.
2. Having finished his homework, Jerry watched TV.
3. The most popular chocolate (being) eaten today is dark chocolate. (passive voice)

Infinitive phrases consist of to+verb, its object, and any modifiers. Infinitives show tense and voice.
1. The play to read for class is Romeo and Juliet.
2. Life is to be enjoyed. passive voice

Prepositional phrases consist of a preposition, its object, and any modifiers.
1. The dog with the spots is a Dalmatian.
2. The President lives in a mansion in Washington D.C.

Discuss adverb equal comparisons.

Discuss adverb phrases.

Describe the function of articles.

Discuss adverb unequal comparisons.

Describe subordinating conjunctions.

Describe coordinating and correlative conjunctions.

Adverb phrases are groups of words used as adverbs.

Prepositional phrases consist of a preposition, its object, and any modifiers.
1. Jonah lived in a whale for a month. how long?
2. Jack and Jill walked to the store. where?
3. They got married after leaving town. when?

Infinitive phrases consist of to+verb, any object, and modifiers.
1. My grandfather left home to sail around the world. why?
2. It costs a lot of money to get a good education. clause modifier

Absolute phrases consist of a participle, its subject, and any modifiers. Absolute phrases modify the entire sentence.
The crowd being totally out of control, the police shot off tear gas.

Equal Comparisons - Use as...as to compare two similar actions.

1. Jane cooks as well as her mother does.

2. The faucet drips as slowly as molasses.

3. He never managed as successfully as his brother did.

4. Citizens are treated as well as non-citizens in Albania.

Unequal Comparisons - Adverbs can be used to compare and contrast dissimilar actions.
Comparative: to compare two actions, use -er/more, less.
Superlative: to refer to the one in a group of three or more that is the outstanding example of the action, use -est/most, least.

One-syllable adverbs use -er/est or less/least
Positive: late
Comparative: later
Superlative: the latest

Two & more syllables use more/most or less/least
Positive: carefully
Comparative: more carefully
Superlative: the most carefully

Irregular Adverbs
Positive: well
Comparative: better
Superlative: the best

Articles (a/an/the) come before a noun and provide important information. "A/an" are often identified as indefinite articles while "the" is identified as the definite article.

Use a/an with singular count nouns to introduce a singular count noun or to discuss all members of a category.

Omit the article with plural count nouns and non-count nouns to indicate some, an indefinite amount; to discuss an abstract non-count noun; and to represent all members of a category.

Use "the" with count nouns and non-count nouns to indicate something that has already been mentioned; to indicate that reader and writer know the something which they refer to; to indicate a noun identified by an adjective phrase or adjective clause; to indicate one of a kind; in science, to represent all members of a category.

Conjunctions join words, phrases, and clauses, showing the relationship between them.

The categories of conjunctions are coordinating, correlative, and subordinating. Conjunctive adverbs or transition words are another type of conjunction.

Coordinating conjunctions join grammatically equal words, phrases, or clauses (two pronouns, two prepositional phrases, two independent clauses, etc.) The coordinating conjunctions are and, but, or, nor.

Correlative conjunctions are used in pairs to join two or more words, phrases, or clauses that are grammatically equal.
Examples:
both...and; not only...but also; either...or; whether...or; neither...nor

Subordinating conjunctions introduce adverbial clauses. They join a dependent adverb clause to an independent clause.

Cause: as, because, since
Comparison: more than, as...as
Conditional: even if, if, unless
Contrast: although, even though, though
Manner: as, as if, as though
Place: where, wherever
Purpose: in order that, so that
Result: so...that
Time: after, before, since, until, when

Describe the function of a noun.

Describe mass, collective, and abstract nouns.

Discuss comparing nouns.

Discuss noun phrases.

Describe the parts of speech.

Describe infinitive, participial, and prepositional phrases.

Mass nouns are concrete nouns that name things that cannot be separated into individual units--snow, sugar, water, air, toothpaste.

Collective nouns identify collections of different kinds of things: equipment, furniture, luggage, traffic. For example, furniture includes chairs, tables, sofas, etc.

Abstract nouns identify qualities, emotions, concepts. Abstract nouns name things that cannot be touched, seen, smelled, heard, or tasted--happiness, anger, love, liberty, equality, democracy. Abstract nouns are not introduced by "the" unless the noun is limited or described in some way--the liberty we cherish.

Nouns name things--persons, places, actions or ideas. Nouns are subjects, direct objects, indirect objects, objects of prepositions, predicate complements and predicate nouns. Nouns also show possession. Most nouns name things that can be counted-one potato, two potatoes, three potatoes. Most count nouns are concrete nouns. They name things that can be touched, seen, smelled, heard, tasted-table, movie, flower, song, candy bar. A/an are used with singular count nouns. "The" is used with both singular and plural count nouns.

Collective count nouns identify groups-family, team, herd, crowd, class. Although these nouns represent a group of individuals, they are understood as one unit and take a singular verb. When they represent two or more groups, they are plural. Most count nouns form the plural by adding "s" Example: toe-toes. Irregular count nouns form the plural in a variety of ways: count nouns ending in "s, sh, x, or z" add "es"; some count nouns change forms; some count nouns stay the same. Non-count nouns name things that can't be counted. Follow these rules. Never add "s" to a non-count noun; always use a singular verb; never use a/an with a non-count noun; never use many with a non-count noun.

Noun phrases are groups of words which act as nouns.

A *gerund phrase* consists of a participle (verb+ing or verb+ed) and its modifiers acting as a noun. Gerunds show tense and voice.
1. Fran hates doing her laundry. direct object
2. Having learned to speak Spanish qualified Jennifer as an interpreter. subject

An *infinitive phrase* consists of to+verb and modifiers or object. Infinitives show tense and voice.
1. To have our own children was always our dream. subject
2. To have met President Reagan would have been a thrill. subject
3. His goal is to become a millionaire. predicate noun

To compare two nouns, use similar to or the same as; to contrast them use different from.

Common noun suffixes (-ance, -ant, -ence, -er, -ism, -ist, -ity, -ment, -ness, -tion, -ship) are often added to other parts of speech to form nouns. They are sometimes even added to other nouns to create new nouns. These suffixes cannot be added at random. When in doubt, check a dictionary.

Verb: commune
Noun: community
Adjective: different
Noun: difference
Noun: account
Noun: accountant

Adjectives, gerunds, infinitives, and prepositions sometimes act as nouns.

A *phrase* is a group of related words acting as one word-a noun, adjective, or adverb.

Infinitives are to+verb. An infinitive phrase is an infinitive plus any objects and modifiers. Infinitives can act as nouns, adjectives or adverbs.

Participles are verb+ing or verb+ed. Participial phrases can function as nouns, adjectives or adverbs. A participle in a phrase shows tense and voice.

When a participle has an object or modifiers and acts as a noun, it is a *gerund phrase*. When a participle has an object or modifiers and acts as an adjective, it is a participial phrase. When a participle has a subject and modifies an entire sentence, it is an absolute phrase.

A *prepositional phrase* consists of a preposition, its object and any modifiers. Prepositional phrases can act as adjectives or adverbs.

An *appositive phrase* identifies or defines the word it follows.

The sentence is the basic unit of communication in English. Parts of speech--*adjectives, adverbs, articles, conjunctions, nouns, pronouns, prepositions, verbs, and interjections*--identify the words which make up a sentence.

Nouns, verbs, adjectives, and adverbs perform essential functions in a sentence and provide the sentence with its content.

Two other parts of speech--conjunctions and prepositions--connect sentences to each other; and, within a sentence, they connect one part--one idea or action--to another.

Some words function only as one part of speech. However, many words can function as two or more parts of speech.

Describe the functions of pronouns, as well as personal pronouns, interrogative pronouns, and relative pronouns.

Describe the function of prepositions, prepositional phrases, and preposition idioms.

Describe the function of a sentence.

Describe demonstrative pronouns, reflexive pronouns, intensive pronouns, and reciprocal pronouns.

Describe the function of a verb.

Describe sentence structure.

Prepositions are connectors. They connect the words which follow them to the rest of the sentence. The most commonly used prepositions are listed below:

about above aboard across after against along among against around at before behind below beneath beside besides between beyond by despite down during except for from in inside into like near of off on out outside over past since through throughout to toward under underneath until up upon with within without

A preposition must be followed by a nominal--a noun, pronoun, gerund, noun phrase, or noun clause.

Prepositional phrases act as adjectives or adverbs.

Idiomatic Use of Prepositions - Some adjectives, nouns, and verbs are always followed by the same preposition--for example, afraid of, agree with.

A *pronoun* always refers back to a noun. That noun is the pronoun's antecedent. Example: She bought some (antecedent) furniture yesterday, but (pronoun) it hasn't arrived. Pronoun and antecedent must agree in number and gender.
Example: We were happy when our (antecedent) relatives came. It was great seeing (pronoun) them.

A *personal pronoun* refers to a person or thing. A personal pronoun can be a subject, an object, or a possessive. Personal pronouns usually change their form depending on if they are used as the subject or object of a sentence.
1st Person: I, we, me, us, mine, ours
2nd Person: you, yours
3rd Person: he, she, it, they, him, her, them, his, hers, theirs

Interrogative pronouns (who, whom, which, what, and whose) ask questions.

Relative pronouns (who, whom, which, that, whose) introduce adjective and noun clauses. The relative pronoun, what, introduces noun clauses only. Within an adjective or noun clause, the relative pronoun can function as a subject, object, or possessive. Relative pronouns of the -ever form (whatever, whichever, whoever, whomever) have an indefinite meaning: they do not refer back to a specific noun.

Demonstrative pronouns (this/these, that/those) indicate distance.
This/these usually indicate nearness in time or space.
That/those usually indicate more distant time and space.
This/that are used with singular nouns. These/those are used with plural nouns.

When the exact quantity or identity of a person, idea or thing, is unknown, use an indefinite pronoun. Although most indefinite pronouns take singular verbs, a few indefinite pronouns take plural verbs and some can take either singular or plural.
Singular Verb: anybody, everyone, something
Plural Verb: few, many, several
Singular/Plural: most, some

Intensive/reflexive pronouns are made by adding -self, -selves to personal pronouns. For example: myself, ourselves. An intensive pronoun emphasizes the noun or pronoun that comes before it. Example: Doug did the work himself.

A reflexive pronoun indicates that the subject and the object of an action are the same person. Example: Ed shot himself in the foot.

Reciprocal pronouns are each other, one another. They refer back to a compound or a plural subject to indicate a relationship.

An English sentence has two parts, the subject and the predicate. The *subject* identifies the topic of the sentence. The *predicate* comments on the topic. The subject must include a noun or a phrase or clause acting as a noun. The predicate must include a verb.
Example: Fred and his wife like to cook.
Subject: Fred and his wife
Predicate: like to cook.

The purpose of a sentence refers to its function. Does the sentence state a fact or an opinion? Does it ask a question? Does it give a command? Does it show excitement?
Declarative – A declarative sentence makes a statement and ends with a period. Example: Animals have their own language. states a fact
Interrogative – An interrogative sentence asks a question and ends with a question mark. Example: Do animals have their own language?
Imperative – An imperative sentence gives a command or makes a request; it ends with a period or an exclamation point. Example: Come with me.
Exclamatory – An exclamatory sentence shows sudden or strong feeling; it ends with an exclamation point. Example: How beautiful she is!

A sentence can be identified according to its structure: simple, compound, complex, or compound-complex.

Every *simple* sentence is an independent clause, which contains a subject and verb, expresses one complete thought, and is grammatically independent. Example: It rained yesterday.

A *compound* sentence has two or more independent clauses joined by a semicolon(;) or by a comma and a coordinating conjunction, such as and, but, or. Example: She likes to eat fruit, and I like to eat vegetables.

A *complex* sentence has one independent clause and at least one dependent clause. The dependent clause is introduced by a relative pronoun (who, which, that, etc.) or a subordinating conjunction (although, because, when, etc.). Example: Because I like to drink milk, my bones are very strong.

A *compound-complex* sentence has two or more independent clauses plus one or more dependent clauses. Example: The plane arrived and we took off, because we were already late.

Verbs state what happens (such as eat or run) or describe a state of being (such as be or appear). All verbs indicate time (hear, heard, will hear; is, was, will be).

All verbs need a subject identifying who or what is acting or being- I think; I am.

Some verbs also have a direct object (He eats meat).

Verbs have five forms: *base form, past tense, past participle, present participle, infinitive.*

Regular verbs form the past tense and the past participle by adding -ed to the base form of the verb (kick, kicked, kicked; walk, walked, walked).

Irregular verbs form the past tense and past participle in many different ways: buy, bought, bought; see, saw, seen.

Describe transitive and intransitive verbs.

Describe linking verbs.

Describe simple present, simple past, and future verb tenses.

Describe present perfect, past perfect, and future perfect verb tenses.

Describe present, past, and future continuous verb tenses.

Describe present, past, and future perfect continuous verb tenses.

Linking verbs do not express action; linking verbs express a state of being. Linking verbs are followed by nouns or adjectives. See examples below:
John was a doctor.
The grapefruit is too sour.

Here is a list of frequently used linking verbs:
Be (am, is, are, was, were, being, been) is the most common linking verb. Sense-related verbs (feel, look, smell, sound, taste) also act as linking verbs.

Some other verbs (appear, become, grow, seem) can also act as linking verbs. An adjective following a linking verb describes the subject. Example: This fruit is really mushy.

A noun following a linking verb renames the subject. See example: He is a doctor.

Some verbs (appear, become, feel, grow, look, smell, sound, and taste) are either linking verbs or action verbs, depending on their meaning in a sentence.
Linking verb: Mary grew ill.
Action verb: We grew tomatoes.

Action verbs tell what happens. They are either transitive (buy, kick, see) or intransitive (walk, fall).

A *transitive verb* is an action verb requiring a direct object (noun, pronoun, noun phrase or clause) to complete its meaning. A transitive verb can also have an indirect object or an objective complement. See examples below:
Mary showed the ring.
Mary showed his mom the ring.
The country elected him President.

An *intransitive verb* is an action verb which can not accept a direct object. An intransitive verb is followed by an adverbial modifier—an adverb, a prepositional phrase—or nothing at all. See examples below:
Fred jumped high.
Fred jumped in the puddle.
Fred jumped.

The *present perfect* tense emphasizes the completion of an action in the very recent past. Example: I have just purchased a necklace.

The *present perfect tense* can also indicate an action begun in the past and continued up to the present moment. See example below:
Sam has lived at the same house for ten years.

The *past perfect* indicates how two finished actions are related in time. The first completed action uses the past perfect while the second action uses the simple past. Example: Before he went blind, Milton had written Paradise Lost.

Future perfect indicates an action to be finished before a future time. Example: I will have finished the book before I take the exam.

Verbs change form to agree with the subject of the action and to indicate the time or tense of the action. Verb tenses can be categorized as simple or perfect. Each of these tenses has a continuous form.

Simple present tense expresses habitual or repeated actions, general truths, future actions, literary or historic present, and states or qualities of being. In statements, do/does expresses emphasis. See examples below:
Susie exercises on Thursdays and Fridays. habitual action
Fred is a doctor. linking verb--state of being

Simple past tense expresses finished actions. Did in statements expresses emphasis. See examples below.
World War II ended in 1945. finished action
Benedict Arnold began as a loyal American, but later he did betray his country. emphasis

Future tense expresses actions or conditions occurring in the future. Simple present tense with an adverb of time can indicate future.
She will see it next week. future tense
The insurance coverage ends next month. simple present

The *present perfect continuous* emphasizes that an action which began in the past will continue into the future. Example: Arlene has been studying music for three years; she still has one more year to go.

The *future perfect continuous* indicates an action continuing until some specific time in the future. Example: He will have been attending school for nineteen years by the time he graduates.

The *past perfect continuous* emphasizes that the first action continued right up to the time of the second action. Example: By the year 2050, people will have been living on Mars for a decade or more.

The *present continuous* expresses ongoing but temporary or future actions. See examples below:
I am riding a bicycle now. ongoing temporary action
She is flying to Australia next summer. future action

Past continuous usually expresses an action in progress at the time of another past action. Example: Sheila was attending a class when the fire alarm went off.

Future continuous expresses a future action. Example: She will be driving to Maine next year.

Discuss active vs. passive verbs.

Describe auxiliary verbs.

Describe verb usage in subjunctive sentences.

Describe verb usage in conditional sentences.

Describe verb patterns.

Describe more detailed verb usage in subjunctive sentences.

Auxiliary verbs (helping verbs and modals) convey important information, but they never work alone. They must combine with a main verb.

Helping verbs combine with a main verb to identify verb tense, number and voice and to introduce questions and form negatives. The helping verbs are be, do, have, will.

Be (am/is/are/was/were/been) helps make the continuous forms and the passive voice.

Continuous forms:
be (am/is/are/was/were/been) + present participle + (verb+ing)
Example:
The girl is running. present continuous
The girl was running. past continuous
The girl has been running. present perfect continuous
The girl had been running. past perfect continuous
Is the girl running? present continuous
Was the girl running? past continuous
Has the girl been running? present perfect continuous
Had the girl been running? past perfect continuous

In an active voice sentence, the subject is the actor. In a passive voice sentence, the opposite is true: the subject is the receiver or the object of the action.
Examples:
Active voice: Mary rocked the baby.
Passive voice: The baby was rocked by Mary.

Only transitive verbs use the passive voice.

The passive voice is formed by using be (am, is, are, was, were, being, been) + past participle.

Verb tense is the key to writing correct conditional and subjunctive sentences.

Conditional sentences express the idea that one situation depends on another. In a conditional sentence, the situation in the independent clause 'your summer begins in January' depends on the situation in the conditional, or 'if,' clause--if you live in Brazil. If, when, whether, and unless introduce conditional sentences. Conditional independent clause: If you live in Brazil, your summer begins in January.

Conditional sentences which express facts, general truths, or habitual actions use the simple present tense in both clauses.
Examples:
If the moon is full, it is hard to see the stars.
When the temperature rises above 85 degrees, we turn on the air conditioning.

Conditional sentences which predict probable actions use the simple present tense in the conditional, or 'if,' clause. The independent clause uses 'will' or a modal.
Example: If it rains tonight, we will cancel the party.

The *subjunctive mood* is used in formal written English to express conditions contrary to fact, wishes, requests, or demands. A key to writing accurate subjunctive sentences is to ignore normal rules of tense and number.

'Condition contrary to fact' describes a situation that does not exist now, never existed, and is unlikely ever to exist; for example, if Thomas Jefferson were alive today or if Thomas Jefferson had been alive during the Civil War.

The 'if clause' uses the past tense; the independent clause uses would/could/might and the base form of the verb. Example: If I were a billionaire, I would buy all the TV networks.

The 'if clause' uses past perfect; the independent clause uses a would/could/might and the present perfect tense. Example: If I had been born in 1900, I would have sailed around the world.
Sentences expressing wishes use the subjunctive in the 'that clause.'

For present tense wishes, use were, the simple past tense, or would/could/might and the simple form of the verb in the 'that clause.'
Example: I wish that the semester were over now.

When a wish is about the past, use the past perfect or would/could/might and the present perfect in the 'that clause.' Example:
He wished that the semester had ended before he ran out of money.

Ask, demand, insist, move, recommend, suggest, and urge followed by 'that clauses' use the simple form of the verb to express both present and past tense. Example: The president asks that everyone work together.

Some verbs are followed by *verbals* (gerunds or infinitives) according to a rigid pattern--want to go but enjoy going. Listed below are the five different patterns.

1. Verb + Infinitive - Napoleon chose to marry Josephine

2. Verb + Gerund - He is enjoying playing tennis these days.

3. Verb + Infinitive or Verb + Gerund - The boy loves going to school.

4. Verb + Object + Verb - She helped him build a house.

5. Verb + Object + Infinitive - They wanted us to teach them to read Spanish.

Discuss capitalization rules for proper nouns.

Describe verbs ending in "ed" or "ing."

Describe miscellaneous capitalization rules.

Describe capitalization rules for titles of persons.

Describe parallelism.

Describe noun-pronoun agreement in number.

When used as adjectives, the past participle (verb+ed) and the present participle (verb+ing) of some verbs have very different meanings. *Psychological verbs* (interest, bore, amuse, etc.) describe emotions or moods. When their participles are used as adjectives, they follow the rules below.

The past participle (verb+ed) describes the person's mental state or inner feelings: the tired student.

The present participle (verb+ing) describes the person or thing which causes the mental state or feelings: the tiring exercises or the tiring speaker.

The most common psychological verbs are: amuse, disappoint, flatter, overwhelm, annoy, disgust, frighten, reassure, bore, encourage, horrify, satisfy, charm, excite, inspire, surprise, confuse, fascinate, interest.

When the participles of action verbs (burn, blow, melt, etc.) are used as adjectives, they follow the rules below.

The past participle (verb+ed) indicates a completed action— melted snow.

The present participle (verb+ing) emphasizes an ongoing process— melting snow.

Action completed: blown hair, boiled water.
Ongoing process: blowing hair, boiling water.

Capitalize *proper nouns* and words formed from proper nouns.

- Capitalize names of *particular persons*: **G**eorge **B**ush, **J**esus **C**hrist.

- Capitalize names of *particular places*, including continents, countries, states, cities, and streets: **A**sia, **C**anada, **W**ashington, **N**ew **Y**ork **C**ity, **P**ennsylvania **A**venue.

- Capitalize names of *particular things*, such as special organizations, holidays, historical events, races and religions, languages, business product brand names, and other particular things such as planets, documents, and monuments: **S**enate, **M**other's **D**ay, **C**ivil **W**ar, **E**nglishman, **C**atholic, **F**ord truck, **V**enus, **D**eclaration of **I**ndependence, and **W**ashington **M**emorial.

- Capitalize words *formed from proper nouns*, such as abbreviations of proper nouns and proper adjectives: **CPA**, **E**nglish.

- Capitalize a common noun or adjective only when it is a *part of a proper name*: Louisiana **S**tate **U**niversity

Capitalize *titles of persons*.

- Capitalize titles when they are used *before a person's name* as part of the name: **P**resident Bush, King David

- Titles *following a name or used alone in place of a name* are not usually capitalized unless used in direct address: the **P**resident of the United States

- Capitalize *family-relationship words* when they are used *before a person's name* and when used *alone in place of the name*: **U**ncle Mike came over for dinner. Hello, **D**ad.

Capitalize the titles of works.

- Capitalize the first and last words and all important words in the titles of *books, magazines, newspapers, poems, stories, plays, and works of art*: **G**one **W**ith the **W**ind (book), **N**ew **Y**ork **Ti**mes (newspaper).

- Capitalize the *first word of every sentence* (including quoted sentences). Patrick Henry said "**G**ive me liberty or give me death."

- Capitalize the pronoun I.

- Capitalize the *first word in every line of poetry*, whether or not the word begins a sentence. See example below:
For though from out our bourne of Time and Place
   The flood may bear me far,
I hope to see my Pilot face to face
   When I have crossed the bar.
                              - Tennyson

A pronoun must agree with its antecedent in *number*. If the antecedent is singular, the pronoun referring to it must be singular; if the antecedent is plural, the pronoun referring to it must be plural.

- Use *singular* pronouns to refer to the singular indefinite pronouns: *each, either, neither, one, everyone, everybody, no one, nobody, anyone, anybody, someone, somebody.*
Example: *Each* of the students bought *their* own lunch. (incorrect)
       Each of the students bought *his* own lunch. (correct)

- Use plural nouns to refer to the plural indefinite pronouns: both, *few, several, many*. Example: *Both* were within *their* boundaries.

- The indefinite pronouns *some, any, none, all, most* may be referred to by *singular* or *plural* pronouns, depending on the sense of the sentence. Examples: *Some* of the children have misplaced *their* toy. (plural)
Some of the carpet has lost *its* nap. (singular)

- Pronouns that refer to compound antecedents joined by *and* are usually plural. Example: Bill and Joe cook *their* own meals.

When a sentence contains a series of items, all the items should be in parallel form. Keeping all phrases and clauses in the same form creates parallelism by clarifying the relationship among the parts of the sentence.

Incorrect: I like running and to swim. (This sentence is not parallel; "running" and "to swim" are not in the same form.

Sentences can be corrected by putting both words in the same form.

Correct: I like running and swimming. (Both words are now in an "–ing" form.

Parallel grammatical structure is important for clear and concise sentences.

Describe negation.

Describe pronoun-noun agreement in gender.

Discuss word usage.

Discuss points to keep in mind while writing an exam essay.

Discuss uses for transitional words and phrases.

Describe various types of paragraphs that can make up the essay body.

A pronoun agrees with its antecedent in gender.

- Antecedents of *masculine* gender (male sex) are referred to by *he, him, his*.

- Antecedents of *feminine* gender (female sex) are referred to by *she, her, hers*.

- Antecedents of *neuter* gender (no sex) are referred to by *it, its*.

- Antecedents of *common* gender (sex not known) are referred to by *he, him, his*. It is understood that the masculine pronouns include both male and female.

- Antecedents that are names of animals are generally referred to by the neuter pronouns unless the writer wishes to indicate special interest in the animal, in which case the masculine pronouns are often used. When a feminine role is naturally suggested, the feminine pronouns are used.

Negation is the process that turns an affirmative statement (I am the walrus) into its opposite denial (I am not the walrus). Nouns as well as verbs can be grammatically negated, by the use of a negative adjective (There is no walrus), a negative pronoun (Nobody is the walrus), or a negative adverb (I never was the walrus). The negative particles are not and no; the negative particle is placed after the auxiliary verb in a sentence.

In English, negation for most verbs other than be and have, or verb phrases in which be, have or do already occur, requires the recasting of the sentence using the dummy auxiliary verb do, which adds little to the meaning of the negative phrase, but serves as a place to attach the negative particles not, or its contracted form -n't, to:
I have a walrus.
I don't have a walrus. (the most common way in contemporary English.)
I do not see the walrus.
I am not seeing the walrus.
I have not seen the walrus.
The verb do also follows this rule, and therefore requires a second instance of itself in order to be marked for negation:
"The walrus doesn't do tricks " not "The walrus doesn't tricks."

1. Clearly announce your position in response to the specified topic and establish the structure of the essay

2. Organize what you plan to write and follow it closely.

3. Be direct and to the point.

4. Provide examples and clear explanations

5. Avoid generalizations.

6. Use transitional phrases to get from one point to another; develop a logical flow between ideas.

7. Use variety in sentence structure; follow rules of standard written English.

8. Save time for revising and editing.

Word usage, or *diction*, refers to the use of words with meanings and forms that are appropriate for the context and structure of a sentence. A common error in word usage occurs when a word's meaning does not fit the context of the sentence.

Incorrect: Susie likes chips better then candy.
Correct: Susie likes chips better than candy.

Incorrect: The cat licked it's coat.
Correct: The cat licked its coat.

Commonly misused words include *than/then, it's/its, there/their/they're, your/you're, except/accept*, and *affect/effect*.

Explanation: give examples, facts, and details

Compare and contrast: discusses how things are similar or different

Chronological: arranged according to timing

Spatial: arranged according to location

Emphasis: arranged in order of importance

Cause and effect: arranged from effect to cause or cause to effect

Problem/solution: arranged according to issues and solutions

Topical: arranged according to topics discussed

Transitional words and phrases can be used to:
1. To add ideas: again; furthermore; besides; too; also

2. To compare or contrast: likewise; yet; however; although

3. To prove: because; since; obviously

4. To show exceptions: yet; however; occasionally

5. To show time: soon; finally; next; then; later

6. To show effect: consequently; thus; therefore

7. To emphasize: obviously; certainly; indeed

8. To give examples: for example; to demonstrate; to illustrate

9. To conclude: thus; consequently; therefore

Discuss the importance of answering the related questions only from the reading.

Discuss drawing conclusions.

Discuss making comparisons and contrasts in the reading passage.

Discuss determining the topic of the reading passage.

Discuss responding to questions regarding predictions of the future.

Discuss contextual clues.

When asked for a *conclusion* that may be drawn, look for critical "hedge" phrases, such as likely, may, can, will often, sometimes, etc, often, almost, mostly, usually, generally, rarely, sometimes.

Question writers insert these hedge phrases, to cover every possibility. Often an answer will be wrong simply because it leaves no room for exception. Extreme positive or negative answers (such as always, never, etc.) are usually not correct.

Your first task when you begin reading is to answer the question "What is the topic of the selection?" This can best be answered by quickly *skimming* the passage for the general idea, stopping to read only the first sentence of each paragraph. A paragraph's first is usually the main topic sentence, and it gives you a summary of the content of the paragraph.

Look for contextual clues. An answer can be right but not correct. The contextual clues will help you find the answer that is most right and is correct. Understand the context in which a phrase is stated.

When asked for the implied meaning of a statement made in the passage, immediately go find the statement and read the context it was made in. Also, look for an answer choice that has a similar phrase to the statement in question.

The reader should not use any outside knowledge that is not gathered from the reading passage to answer the related questions. Correct answers can be derived straight from the reading passage.

The author will often present *comparisons* and *contrasts* in the reading passage. These are often couples with signal words, such as: more, most, less, least, but, or, instead, then-now, and before-after.

To respond to questions requiring future predictions, base your answers on evidence of past or present behavior.

Reading Comprehension

© Mometrix Media - flashcardsecrets.com/toefl
TOEFL Essentials

Describe the following words: aberrant, aberration, abet, abeyance, abjure.

Reading Comprehension

© Mometrix Media - flashcardsecrets.com/toefl
TOEFL Essentials

Describe the following words: ablution, abrogate, abscond, abstemious, abstruse.

Reading Comprehension

© Mometrix Media - flashcardsecrets.com/toefl
TOEFL Essentials

Describe the following words: abut, accede, acquiesce, acrid, acumen.

Reading Comprehension

© Mometrix Media - flashcardsecrets.com/toefl
TOEFL Essentials

Describe the following words: adage, adamant, admonition, adumbrate, affable.

Reading Comprehension

© Mometrix Media - flashcardsecrets.com/toefl
TOEFL Essentials

Describe the following words: aggrandize, aggravate, agile, agog, alacrity.

Reading Comprehension

© Mometrix Media - flashcardsecrets.com/toefl
TOEFL Essentials

Describe the following words: alcove, alleviate, aloof, amalgamate, ambidextrous.

ablution: A washing or cleansing, especially of the body.

abrogate: To abolish, repeal.

abscond: To depart suddenly and secretly, as for the purpose of escaping arrest.

abstemious: Characterized by self denial or abstinence, as in the use of drink, food.

abstruse: Dealing with matters difficult to be understood.

aberrant: Markedly different from an accepted norm.

aberration: Deviation from a right, customary, or prescribed course.

abet: To aid, promote, or encourage the commission of (an offense).

abeyance: A state of suspension or temporary inaction.

abjure: To recant, renounce, repudiate under oath.

adage: An old saying.

adamant: Any substance of exceeding hardness or impenetrability.

admonition: Gentle reproof.

adumbrate: To represent beforehand in outline or by emblem.

affable: Easy to approach.

abut: To touch at the end or boundary line.

accede: To agree.

acquiesce: To comply; submit.

acrid: Harshly pungent or bitter.

acumen: Quickness of intellectual insight, or discernment; keenness of discrimination.

alcove: A covered recess connected with or at the side of a larger room.

alleviate: To make less burdensome or less hard to bear.

aloof: Not in sympathy with or desiring to associate with others.

amalgamate: To mix or blend together in a homogeneous body.

ambidextrous: Having the ability of using both hands with equal skill or ease.

aggrandize: To cause to appear greatly.

aggravate: To make heavier, worse, or more burdensome.

agile: Able to move or act quickly, physically, or mentally.

agog: In eager desire.

alacrity: Cheerful willingness.

Describe the following words: ambiguous, ameliorate, anathema, animadversion, animosity.

Describe the following words: antediluvian, antidote, aplomb, Apocryphal, apogee.

Describe the following words: apostate, apotheosis, apparition, appease, apposite.

Describe the following words: apprise, approbation, arboreal, ardor, argot.

Describe the following words: arrant, ascetic, ascribe, asperity, assiduous.

Describe the following words: assuage, astringent, astute, atonement, audacious.

antediluvian: Of or pertaining to the times, things, events before the great flood in the days of Noah.

antidote: Anything that will counteract or remove the effects of poison, disease, or the like.

aplomb: Confidence; coolness.

apocryphal: Of doubtful authority or authenticity.

apogee: The climax.

ambiguous: Having a double meaning.

ameliorate: To relieve, as from pain or hardship

anathema: Anything forbidden, as by social usage.

animadversion: The utterance of criticism or censure.

animosity: Hatred.

apprise: To give notice to; to inform.

approbation: Sanction.

arboreal: Of or pertaining to a tree or trees.

ardor: Intensity of passion or affection.

argot: A specialized vocabulary peculiar to a particular group.

apostate: False.

apotheosis: Deification.

apparition: Ghost.

appease: To soothe by quieting anger or indignation.

apposite: Appropriate.

assuage: To cause to be less harsh, violent, or severe, as excitement, appetite, pain, or disease.

astringent: Harsh in disposition or character.

astute: Keen in discernment.

atonement: Amends, reparation, or expiation made from wrong or injury.

audacious: Fearless.

arrant: Notoriously bad.

ascetic: Given to severe self-denial and practicing excessive abstinence and devotion.

ascribe: To assign as a quality or attribute.

asperity: Harshness or roughness of temper.

assiduous: Unceasing; persistent

Describe the following words: augury, auspicious, austere, autocrat, auxiliary.

Describe the following words: avarice, aver, aversion, avow, baleful.

Describe the following words: banal, bask, beatify, bedaub, bellicose.

Describe the following words: belligerent, benefactor, benevolence, benign, berate.

Describe the following words: bewilder, blandishment, blatant, blithe, boisterous.

Describe the following words: bolster, bombast, boorish, breach, brittle.

avarice: Passion for getting and keeping riches.

aver: To avouch, justify or prove

aversion: A mental condition of fixed opposition to or dislike of some particular thing.

avow: To declare openly.

baleful: Malignant.

augury: Omen

auspicious: Favorable omen

austere: Severely simple; unadorned.

autocrat: Any one who claims or wields unrestricted or undisputed authority or influence.

auxiliary: One who or that which aids or helps, especially when regarded as subsidiary or accessory.

belligerent: Manifesting a warlike spirit.

benefactor: A doer of kindly and charitable acts.

benevolence: Any act of kindness or well-doing.

benign: Good and kind of heart.

berate: To scold severely.

banal: Commonplace.

bask: To make warm by genial heat.

beatify: To make supremely happy.

bedaub: To smear over, as with something oily or sticky.

bellicose: Warlike.

bolster: To support, as something wrong.

bombast: Inflated or extravagant language, especially on unimportant subjects.

boorish: Rude.

breach: The violation of official duty, lawful right, or a legal obligation.

brittle: Fragile.

bewilder: To confuse the perceptions or judgment of.

blandishment: Flattery intended to persuade.

blatant: Noisily or offensively loud or clamorous.

blithe: Joyous.

boisterous: Unchecked merriment or animal spirits.

Reading Comprehension
© Mometrix Media - flashcardsecrets.com/toefl
TOEFL Essentials

Describe the following words: broach, bumptious, buoyant, burnish, cabal.

Reading Comprehension
© Mometrix Media - flashcardsecrets.com/toefl
TOEFL Essentials

Describe the following words: cacophony, cajole, callow, calumny, candid.

Reading Comprehension
© Mometrix Media - flashcardsecrets.com/toefl
TOEFL Essentials

Describe the following words: cant, capacious, capitulate, captious, castigate.

Reading Comprehension
© Mometrix Media - flashcardsecrets.com/toefl
TOEFL Essentials

Describe the following words: cataract, caustic, censure, centurion, chagrin.

Reading Comprehension
© Mometrix Media - flashcardsecrets.com/toefl
TOEFL Essentials

Describe the following words: chary, chicanery, circumlocution, coddle, coerce.

Reading Comprehension
© Mometrix Media - flashcardsecrets.com/toefl
TOEFL Essentials

Describe the following words: coeval, cogent, cogitate, cognizant, colloquial.

cacophony: A disagreeable, harsh, or discordant sound or combination of sounds or tones.

cajole: To impose on or dupe by flattering speech.

callow: Without experience of the world.

calumny: Slander.

candid: Straightforward.

broach: To mention, for the first time.

bumptious: Full of offensive and aggressive self-conceit.

buoyant: Having the power or tendency to float or keep afloat.

burnish: To make brilliant or shining.

cabal: A number of persons secretly united for effecting by intrigue some private purpose.

cataract: Opacity of the lens of the eye resulting in complete or partial blindness.

caustic: Sarcastic and severe.

censure: To criticize severely; also, an expression of disapproval.

centurion: A captain of a company of one hundred infantry in the ancient Roman army.

chagrin: Keen vexation, annoyance, or mortification, as at one's failures or errors.

cant: To talk in a singsong, preaching tone with affected solemnity.

capacious: Roomy.

capitulate: To surrender or stipulate terms.

captious: Hypercritical.

castigate: To punish.

coeval: Existing during the same period of time; also, a contemporary.

cogent: Appealing strongly to the reason or conscience.

cogitate: Consider carefully and deeply; ponder.

cognizant: Taking notice.

colloquial: Pertaining or peculiar to common speech as distinguished from literary.

chary: Careful; wary; cautious.

chicanery: The use of trickery to deceive.

circumlocution: Indirect or roundabout expression.

coddle: To treat as a baby or an invalid.

coerce: To force.

Describe the following words: collusion, comestible, commemorate, complaisance, complement.

Describe the following words: comport, compunction, conceit, conciliatory, concord.

Describe the following words: concur, condense, conflagration, confluence, congeal.

Describe the following words: conjoin, connoisseur, console, conspicuous, consternation.

Describe the following words: constrict, consummate, contiguous, contrite, contumacious.

Describe the following words: copious, cornucopia, corporeal, correlate, corroboration.

comport: To conduct or behave (oneself).

compunction: Remorseful feeling.

conceit: Self-flattering opinion.

conciliatory: Tending to reconcile.

concord: Harmony.

collusion: A secret agreement for a wrongful purpose.

comestible: Fit to be eaten.

commemorate: To serve as a remembrance of.

complaisance: Politeness.

complement: To make complete.

conjoin: To unite.

connoisseur: A critical judge of art, especially one with thorough knowledge and sound judgment of art.

console: To comfort.

conspicuous: Clearly visible.

consternation: Panic

concur: To agree.

condense: To abridge.

conflagration: A great fire, as of many buildings, a forest, or the like.

confluence: The place where streams meet.

congeal: To coagulate.

copious: Plenteous.

cornucopia: The horn of plenty, symbolizing peace and prosperity.

corporeal: Of a material nature; physical.

correlate: To put in some relation of connection or correspondence.

corroboration: Confirmation.

constrict: To bind.

consummate: To bring to completion.

contiguous: Touching or joining at the edge or boundary.

contrite: Broken in spirit because of a sense of sin.

contumacious: Rebellious.

Describe the following words: counterfeit, countervail, covert, cower, crass.

Describe the following words: credulous, cupidity, cursory, curtail, cynosure.

Describe the following words: dearth, defer, deign, deleterious, delineate.

Describe the following words: deluge, demagogue, denizen, denouement, deplete.

Describe the following words: deposition, deprave, deprecate, deride, derision.

Describe the following words: derivative, descry, desiccant, desuetude, desultory.

credulous: Easily deceived.

cupidity: Avarice.

cursory: Rapid and superficial.

curtail: To cut off or cut short.

cynosure: That to which general interest or attention is directed.

counterfeit: Made to resemble something else.

countervail: To offset.

covert: Concealed, especially for an evil purpose.

cower: To crouch down tremblingly, as through fear or shame.

crass: Coarse or thick in nature or structure, as opposed to thin or fine.

deluge: To overwhelm with a flood of water.

demagogue: An unprincipled politician.

denizen: Inhabitant.

denouement: That part of a play or story in which the mystery is cleared up.

deplete: To reduce or lessen, as by use, exhaustion, or waste.

dearth: Scarcity, as of something customary, essential, or desirable.

defer: To delay or put off to some other time.

deign: To deem worthy of notice or account.

deleterious: Hurtful, morally or physically.

delineate: To represent by sketch or diagram.

derivative: Coming or acquired from some origin.

descry: To discern.

desiccant: Any remedy which, when applied externally, dries up or absorbs moisture, as that of wounds.

desuetude: A state of disuse or inactivity.

desultory: Not connected with what precedes.

deposition: Testimony legally taken on interrogatories and reduced to writing, for use as evidence in court.

deprave: To render bad, especially morally bad.

deprecate: To express disapproval or regret for, with hope for the opposite.

deride: To ridicule.

derision: Ridicule.

Describe the following words: deter, dexterity, diaphanous, diatribe, didactic.

Describe the following words: diffidence, diffident, dilate, dilatory, disallow.

Describe the following words: discomfit, disconcert, disconsolate, discountenance, discredit.

Describe the following words: discreet, disheveled, dissemble, disseminate, dissent.

Describe the following words: dissolution, distraught, divulge, dogmatic, dormant.

Describe the following words: dubious, duplicity, earthenware, ebullient, edacious.

diffidence: Self-distrust.

diffident: Affected or possessed with self-distrust.

dilate: To enlarge in all directions.

dilatory: Tending to cause delay.

disallow: To withhold permission or sanction.

deter: To frighten away.

dexterity: Readiness, precision, efficiency, and ease in any physical activity or in any mechanical work.

diaphanous: Transparent.

diatribe: A bitter or malicious criticism.

didactic: Pertaining to teaching.

discreet: Judicious.

disheveled: Disordered; disorderly; untidy.

dissemble: To hide by pretending something different.

disseminate: To sow or scatter abroad, as seed is sown.

dissent: Disagreement.

discomfit: To put to confusion.

disconcert: To disturb the composure of.

disconsolate : Hopelessly sad; also, saddening; cheerless.

discountenance: To look upon with disfavor.

discredit: To injure the reputation of.

dubious: Doubtful.

duplicity: Double-dealing.

earthenware: Anything made of clay and baked in a kiln or dried in the sun.

ebullient: Showing enthusiasm or exhilaration of feeling.

edacious: Given to eating.

dissolution: A breaking up of a union of persons.

distraught: Bewildered.

divulge: To tell or make known, as something previously private or secret.

dogmatic: Making statements without argument or evidence.

dormant: Being in a state of or resembling sleep.

Describe the following words: edible, educe, effete, efficacy, effrontery.

Describe the following words: effulgence, egregious, egress, elegy, elicit.

Describe the following words: elucidate, emaciate, embellish, embezzle, emblazon.

Describe the following words: encomium, encumbrance, endemic, enervate, engender.

Describe the following words: engrave, enigma, enmity, entangle, entreat.

Describe the following words: Epicurean, epithet, epitome, equable, equanimity.

effulgence: Splendor.

egregious: Extreme.

egress: Any place of exit.

elegy: A lyric poem lamenting the dead.

elicit: To educe or extract gradually or without violence.

edible: Suitable to be eaten.

educe: To draw out.

effete: Exhausted, as having performed its functions.

efficacy: The power to produce an intended effect as shown in the production of it.

effrontery: Unblushing impudence.

encomium: A formal or discriminating expression of praise.

encumbrance: A burdensome and troublesome load.

endemic: Peculiar to some specified country or people.

enervate: To render ineffective or inoperative.

engender: To produce.

elucidate: To bring out more clearly the facts concerning.

emaciate: To waste away in flesh.

embellish: To make beautiful or elegant by adding attractive or ornamental features.

embezzle: To misappropriate secretly.

emblazon: To set forth publicly or in glowing terms.

Epicurean: Indulging, ministering, or pertaining to daintiness of appetite.

epithet: Word used adjectivally to describe some quality or attribute of is objects, as in "Father Aeneas".

epitome: A simplified representation.

equable: Equal and uniform; also, serene.

equanimity: Evenness of mind or temper.

engrave: To cut or carve in or upon some surface.

enigma: A riddle.

enmity: Hatred.

entangle: To involve in difficulties, confusion, or complications.

entreat: To ask for or request earnestly.

Describe the following words: equanimity, equilibrium, equivocal, equivocate, eradicate.

Describe the following words: errant, erratic, erroneous, erudite, eschew.

Describe the following words: espy, eulogy, euphonious, evanescent, evince.

Describe the following words: evoke, exacerbate, exculpate, exhaustive, exigency.

Describe the following words: exigency, exorbitant, expatiate, expedient, expiate.

Describe the following words: explicate, expostulate, expropriate, extant, extempore.

errant: Roving or wandering, as in search of adventure or opportunity for gallant deeds.

erratic: Irregular.

erroneous: Incorrect.

erudite: Very-learned.

eschew: To keep clear of.

equanimity: Calmness; composure.

equilibrium: A state of balance.

equivocal: Ambiguous.

equivocate: To use words of double meaning.

eradicate: To destroy thoroughly.

evoke: To call or summon forth.

exacerbate: To make more sharp, severe, or virulent.

exculpate: To relieve of blame.

exhaustive: Thorough and complete in execution.

exigency: A critical period or condition.

espy: To keep close watch.

eulogy: A spoken or written laudation of a person's life or character.

euphonious: Characterized by agreeableness of sound.

evanescent: Fleeting.

evince: To make manifest or evident.

explicate: To clear from involvement.

expostulate: To discuss.

expropriate: To deprive of possession; also, to transfer (another's property) to oneself.

extant: Still existing and known.

extempore: Without studied or special preparation.

exigency: State of requiring immediate action; also, an urgent situation; also, that which is required in a

exorbitant: Going beyond usual and proper limits.

expatiate: To speak or write at some length.

expedient: Contributing to personal advantage.

expiate: To make satisfaction or amends for.

Describe the following words: extenuate, extinct, extinguish, extirpate, extol.

Describe the following words: extort, extraneous, exuberance, facetious, facile.

Describe the following words: factious, fallacious, fatuous, fawn, feint.

Describe the following words: felon, ferocity, fervid, fervor, fidelity.

Describe the following words: finesse, flamboyant, flippant, florid, flout.

Describe the following words: foible, foment, foppish, forbearance, forfeit.

extort: To obtain by violence, threats, compulsion, or the subjection of another to some necessity.

extraneous: Having no essential relation to a subject.

exuberance: Rich supply.

facetious: Amusing.

facile: Not difficult to do.

extenuate: To diminish the gravity or importance of.

extinct: Being no longer in existence.

extinguish: To render extinct.

extirpate: To root out; to eradicate.

extol: To praise in the highest terms.

felon: A criminal or depraved person.

ferocity: Savageness.

fervid: Intense.

fervor: Ardor or intensity of feeling.

fidelity: Loyalty.

factious: Turbulent.

fallacious: Illogical.

fatuous: Idiotic

fawn: A young deer.

feint: Any sham, pretense, or deceptive movement.

foible: A personal weakness or failing.

foment: To nurse to life or activity; to encourage.

foppish: Characteristic of one who is unduly devoted to dress and the niceties of manners.

forbearance: Patient endurance or toleration of offenses.

forfeit: To lose possession of through failure to fulfill some obligation.

finesse: Subtle contrivance used to gain a point.

flamboyant: Characterized by extravagance and in general by want of good taste.

flippant: Having a light, pert, trifling disposition.

florid: Flushed with red.

flout: To treat with contempt.

Reading Comprehension
© Mometrix Media - flashcardsecrets.com/toefl
TOEFL Essentials

Describe the following words: forgery, forswear, fragile, frantic, frugal.

Reading Comprehension
© Mometrix Media - flashcardsecrets.com/toefl
TOEFL Essentials

Describe the following words: fugacious, fulminate, fulsome, gainsay, gamut.

Reading Comprehension
© Mometrix Media - flashcardsecrets.com/toefl
TOEFL Essentials

Describe the following words: garrulous, germane, gesticulate, glimmer, gossamer.

Reading Comprehension
© Mometrix Media - flashcardsecrets.com/toefl
TOEFL Essentials

Describe the following words: gourmand, grandiloquent, gregarious, grievous, guile.

Reading Comprehension
© Mometrix Media - flashcardsecrets.com/toefl
TOEFL Essentials

Describe the following words: gullible, halcyon, harangue, harbinger, head.

Reading Comprehension
© Mometrix Media - flashcardsecrets.com/toefl
TOEFL Essentials

Describe the following words: heinous, heresy, heterogeneous, hirsute, hoodwink.

fugacious: Fleeting.

fulminate: To cause to explode.

fulsome: Offensive from excess of praise or commendation.

gainsay: To contradict; to deny.

gamut: The whole range or sequence.

forgery: Counterfeiting.

forswear: To renounce upon oath.

fragile: Easily broken.

frantic: Frenzied.

frugal: Economical.

gourmand: A connoisseur in the delicacies of the table.

grandiloquent: Speaking in or characterized by a pompous or bombastic style.

gregarious: Sociable, outgoing

grievous: Creating affliction.

guile: Duplicity.

garrulous: Given to constant trivial talking.

germane: Relevant.

gesticulate: To make gestures or motions, as in speaking, or in place of speech.

glimmer: A faint, wavering, unsteady light.

gossamer: Flimsy

heinous: Odiously sinful.

heresy: An opinion or doctrine subversive of settled beliefs or accepted principles.

heterogeneous: Consisting of dissimilar elements or ingredients of different kinds.

hirsute: Having a hairy covering.

hoodwink: To deceive.

gullible: Credulous.

halcyon: Calm.

harangue: A tirade.

harbinger: One who or that which foreruns and announces the coming of any person or thing.

head: Adv. Precipitately, as in diving.

Describe the following words: hospitable, hypocrisy, iconoclast, idiosyncrasy, ignoble.

Describe the following words: ignominious, illicit, imbroglio, imbue, immaculate.

Describe the following words: imminent, immutable, impair, impassive, impecunious.

Describe the following words: impede, imperative, imperious, imperturbable, impervious.

Describe the following words: impetuous, impiety, implacable, implicate, implicit.

Describe the following words: importunate, importune, impromptu, improvident, impugn.

ignominious: Shameful.

illicit: Unlawful.

imbroglio: A misunderstanding attended by ill feeling, perplexity, or strife.

imbue: To dye; to instill profoundly.

immaculate: Without spot or blemish.

hospitable: Disposed to treat strangers or guests with generous kindness.

hypocrisy: Extreme insincerity.

iconoclast: An image-breaker.

idiosyncrasy: A mental quality or habit peculiar to an individual.

ignoble: Low in character or purpose.

impede: To be an obstacle or to place obstacles in the way of.

imperative: Obligatory.

imperious: Insisting on obedience.

imperturbable: Calm.

impervious: Impenetrable.

imminent: Dangerous and close at hand.

immutable: Unchangeable.

impair: To cause to become less or worse.

impassive: Unmoved by or not exhibiting feeling.

impecunious: Having no money

importunate: Urgent in character, request, or demand.

importune: To harass with persistent demands or entreaties.

impromptu: Anything done or said on the impulse of the moment.

improvident: Lacking foresight or thrift.

impugn: To assail with arguments, insinuations, or accusations.

impetuous: Impulsive.

impiety: Irreverence toward God.

implacable: Incapable of being pacified.

implicate: To show or prove to be involved in or concerned

implicit: Implied.

Describe the following words: impute, inadvertent, inane, incessant, inchoate.

Describe the following words: incipient, incite, incongruous, inculcate, indelible.

Describe the following words: indigence, indigenous, indistinct, indolence, indolent.

Describe the following words: indomitable, indulgent, ineffable, ineluctable, inept.

Describe the following words: inexorable, infuse, ingenuous, inimical, innocuous.

Describe the following words: inscrutable, insensible, insinuate, insipid, insouciant.

incipient: Initial.

incite: To rouse to a particular action.

incongruous: Unsuitable for the time, place, or occasion.

inculcate: To teach by frequent repetitions.

indelible: That cannot be blotted out, effaced, destroyed, or removed.

impute: To attribute.

inadvertent: Accidental.

inane: Silly.

incessant: Unceasing.

inchoate: Incipient.

indomitable: Unconquerable.

indulgent: Yielding to the desires or humor of oneself or those under one's care.

ineffable: Unutterable.

ineluctable: Impossible to avoid.

inept: Not fit or suitable.

indigence: Poverty.

indigenous: Native.

indistinct: Vague.

indolence: Laziness.

indolent: Habitually inactive or idle.

inscrutable: Impenetrably mysterious or profound.

insensible: Imperceptible.

insinuate: To imply.

insipid: Tasteless.

insouciant: Nonchalant.

inexorable: Unrelenting.

infuse: To instill, introduce, or inculcate, as principles or qualities.

ingenuous: Candid, frank, or open in character or quality.

inimical: Adverse.

innocuous: Harmless.

Describe the following words: insurrection, interdict, interim, intransigent, intrepid.

Describe the following words:, introspection, inundate, inure, invalid, invective.

Describe the following words: inveigh, inveterate, invidious, invincible, iota.

Describe the following words: irascible, irate, ire, irksome, itinerant.

Describe the following words: itinerate, jocular, jovial, judicious, junta.

Describe the following words: lachrymose, lackadaisical, languid, lascivious, lassitude.

introspection: The act of observing and analyzing one's own thoughts and feelings.

inundate: To fill with an overflowing abundance.

inure: To harden or toughen by use, exercise, or exposure.

invalid: One who is disabled by illness or injury.

invective: An utterance intended to cast censure, or reproach.

insurrection: The state of being in active resistance to authority.

interdict: Authoritative act of prohibition.

interim: Time between acts or periods.

intransigent: Not capable of being swayed or diverted from a course.

intrepid: Fearless and bold.

irascible: Prone to anger.

irate: Moved to anger.

ire: Wrath.

irksome: Wearisome.

itinerant: Wandering.

inveigh: To utter vehement censure or invective.

inveterate: Habitual.

invidious: Showing or feeling envy.

invincible: Not to be conquered, subdued, or overcome.

iota: A small or insignificant mark or part.

lachrymose: Given to shedding tears.

lackadaisical: Listless.

languid: Relaxed.

lascivious: Lustful.

lassitude: Lack of vitality or energy.

itinerate: To wander from place to place.

jocular: Inclined to joke.

jovial: Merry.

judicious: Prudent.

junta: A council or assembly that deliberates in secret upon the affairs of government.

Describe the following words: latent, laudable, laudatory, legacy, levee.

Describe the following words: levity, lexicon, libel, licentious, lien.

Describe the following words: listless, lithe, loquacious, lugubrious, luminary.

Describe the following words: lustrous, malaise, malcontent, malevolence, malign.

Describe the following words: malleable, massacre, maudlin, mawkish, mellifluous.

Describe the following words: mendacious, mendicant, meretricious, mesmerize, meticulous.

levity: Frivolity.

lexicon: A dictionary.

libel: Defamation.

licentious: Wanton.

lien: A legal claim or hold on property, as security for a debt or charge.

latent: Dormant.

laudable: Praiseworthy.

laudatory: Pertaining to, expressing, or containing praise.

legacy: A bequest.

levee: An embankment beside a river or stream or an arm of the sea, to prevent overflow.

lustrous: Shining.

malaise: A condition of uneasiness or ill-being.

malcontent: One who is dissatisfied with the existing state of affairs.

malevolence: Ill will.

malign: To speak evil of, especially to do so falsely and severely.

listless: Inattentive

lithe: Supple.

loquacious: Talkative.

lugubrious: Indicating sorrow, often ridiculously.

luminary: One of the heavenly bodies as a source of light.

mendacious: Untrue.

mendicant: A beggar.

meretricious: Alluring by false or gaudy show.

mesmerize: To hypnotize.

meticulous: Over-cautious.

malleable: Pliant.

massacre: The unnecessary and indiscriminate killing of human beings.

maudlin: Foolishly and tearfully affectionate.

mawkish: Sickening or insipid.

mellifluous: Sweetly or smoothly flowing.

Describe the following words: mettle, mettlesome, microcosm, mien, mischievous.

Describe the following words: miscreant, miser, misnomer, moderation, modicum.

Describe the following words: mollify, molt, monomania, morbid, mordant.

Describe the following words: moribund, morose, multifarious, mundane, munificent.

Describe the following words: myriad, nadir, nefarious, negligent, neophyte.

Describe the following words: noisome, nostrum, noxious, nugatory, obdurate.

miscreant: A villain.

miser: A person given to saving and hoarding unduly.

misnomer: A name wrongly or mistakenly applied.

moderation: Temperance.

modicum: A small or token amount.

mettle: Courage.

mettlesome: Having courage or spirit.

microcosm: The world or universe on a small scale.

mien: The external appearance or manner of a person.

mischievous: Fond of tricks.

moribund: On the point of dying.

morose: Gloomy.

multifarious: Having great diversity or variety.

mundane: Worldly, as opposed to spiritual or celestial.

munificent: Extraordinarily generous.

mollify: To soothe.

molt: To cast off, as hair, feathers, etc.

monomania: The unreasonable pursuit of one idea.

morbid: Caused by or denoting a diseased or unsound condition of body or mind.

mordant: Biting.

noisome: Very offensive, particularly to the sense of smell.

nostrum: Any scheme or recipe of a charlatan character.

noxious. Hurtful.

nugatory: Having no power or force.

obdurate: Impassive to feelings of humanity or pity.

myriad: A vast indefinite number.

nadir: The lowest point.

nefarious: Wicked in the extreme.

negligent: Apt to omit what ought to be done.

neophyte: Having the character of a beginner.

Describe the following words: obfuscate, oblique, obsequious, obstreperous, obtrude.

Describe the following words: obtrusive, obviate, odious, odium, officious.

Describe the following words: ominous, onerous, onus, opprobrium, ossify.

Describe the following words: ostentation, ostracism, ostracize, palate, palatial.

Describe the following words: palliate, palpable, panacea, panegyric, panoply.

Describe the following words: paragon, Pariah, paroxysm, parsimonious, partisan.

obtrusive: Tending to be pushed or to push oneself into undue prominence.

obviate: To clear away or provide for, as an objection or difficulty.

odious: Hateful.

odium: A feeling of extreme repugnance, or of dislike and disgust.

officious: Intermeddling with what is not one's concern.

obfuscate: To darken; to obscure.

oblique: Slanting; said of lines.

obsequious: Showing a servile readiness to fall in with the wishes or will of another.

obstreperous: Boisterous.

obtrude: To be pushed or to push oneself into undue prominence.

ostentation: A display dictated by vanity and intended to invite applause or flattery.

ostracism: Exclusion from intercourse or favor, as in society or politics.

ostracize: To exclude from public or private favor.

palate: The roof of the mouth.

palatial: Magnificent.

ominous: Portentous.

onerous: Burdensome or oppressive.

onus: A burden or responsibility.

opprobrium: The state of being scornfully reproached or accused of evil.

ossify: To convert into bone.

paragon: A model of excellence.

Pariah: A member of a degraded class; a social outcast.

paroxysm: A sudden outburst of any kind of activity.

parsimonious: Unduly sparing in the use or expenditure of money.

partisan: Characterized by or exhibiting undue or unreasoning devotion to a party.

palliate: To cause to appear less guilty.

palpable: Perceptible by feeling or touch.

panacea: A remedy or medicine proposed for or professing to cure all diseases.

panegyric: A formal and elaborate eulogy, written or spoken, of a person or of an act.

panoply: A full set of armor.

Describe the following words: pathos, paucity, peccadillo, pedestrian, pellucid.

Describe the following words: penchant, penurious, penury, peregrination, peremptory.

Describe the following words: perfidy, perfunctory, peripatetic, perjury, permeate.

Describe the following words: pernicious, persiflage, perspicacity, perturbation, petrify.

Describe the following words: petulant, phlegmatic, physiognomy, pious, pique,

Describe the following words: placate, platitude, plea, plenary, plethora,

penchant: A bias in favor of something.

penurious: Excessively sparing in the use of money.

penury: Indigence.

peregrination: A wandering.

peremptory: Precluding question or appeal.

pathos: The quality in any form of representation that rouses emotion or sympathy.

paucity: Fewness.

peccadillo: A small breach of propriety or principle.

pedestrian: One who journeys on foot.

pellucid: Translucent.

pernicious: Tending to kill or hurt.

persiflage: Banter.

perspicacity: Acuteness or discernment.

perturbation: Mental excitement or confusion.

petrify: To convert into a substance of stony hardness and character.

perfidy: Treachery.

perfunctory: Half-hearted.

peripatetic: Walking about.

perjury: A solemn assertion of a falsity.

permeate: To pervade.

placate: To bring from a state of angry or hostile feeling to one of patience or friendliness.

platitude: A written or spoken statement that is flat, dull, or commonplace.

plea: An argument to obtain some desired action.

plenary: Entire.

plethora: Excess; superabundance

petulant: Displaying impatience.

phlegmatic: Not easily roused to feeling or action.

physiognomy: The external appearance merely.

pious: Religious.

pique: To excite a slight degree of anger in.

Reading Comprehension
© Mometrix Media - flashcardsecrets.com/toefl
TOEFL Essentials

Describe the following words: plumb, plummet, poignant, polyglot, ponderous.

Reading Comprehension
© Mometrix Media - flashcardsecrets.com/toefl
TOEFL Essentials

Describe the following words: portend, portent, precarious, preclude, precocious.

Reading Comprehension
© Mometrix Media - flashcardsecrets.com/toefl
TOEFL Essentials

Describe the following words: predominate, premature, presage, prescience, presumption.

Reading Comprehension
© Mometrix Media - flashcardsecrets.com/toefl
TOEFL Essentials

Describe the following words: preternatural, prevalent, prevaricate, prim, pristine.

Reading Comprehension
© Mometrix Media - flashcardsecrets.com/toefl
TOEFL Essentials

Describe the following words: probity, proclivity, procrastination, prodigal, prodigious.

Reading Comprehension
© Mometrix Media - flashcardsecrets.com/toefl
TOEFL Essentials

Describe the following words: profligacy, profligate, profuse, prolix, propinquity.

portend: To indicate as being about to happen, especially by previous signs.

portent: Anything that indicates what is to happen.

precarious: Perilous.

preclude: To prevent.

precocious: Having the mental faculties prematurely developed.

plumb: A weight suspended by a line to test the verticality of something.

plummet: A piece of lead for making soundings, adjusting walls to the vertical.

poignant: Severely painful or acute to the spirit.

polyglot: Speaking several tongues.

ponderous: Unusually weighty or forcible.

preternatural: Extraordinary.

prevalent: Of wide extent or frequent occurrence.

prevaricate: To use ambiguous or evasive language for the purpose of deceiving or diverting attention.

prim: Stiffly proper.

pristine: Primitive.

predominate: To be chief in importance, quantity, or degree.

premature: Coming too soon.

presage: To foretell.

prescience: Knowledge of events before they take place.

presumption: That which may be logically assumed to be true until disproved.

profligacy: Shameless viciousness.

profligate: Recklessly wasteful

profuse: Produced or displayed in overabundance.

prolix: Verbose.

propinquity: Nearness.

probity: Virtue or integrity tested and confirmed.

proclivity: A natural inclination.

procrastination: Delay.

prodigal: One wasteful or extravagant, especially in the use of money or property.

prodigious: Immense.

Describe the following words: propitious, prosaic, proscribe, protuberant, provident.

Describe the following words: prudence, puerile, pugnacious, punctilious, pungency.

Describe the following words: pusillanimous, pyre, qualm, quandary, quibble.

Describe the following words: quiescence, quiescent, Quixotic, quotidian, raconteur.

Describe the following words: ramify, rapacious, raucous, reactionary, rebuff.

Describe the following words: recalcitrant, recant, reciprocity, recluse, recondite.

prudence: Caution.

puerile: Childish.

pugnacious: Quarrelsome.

punctilious: Strictly observant of the rules or forms prescribed by law or custom.

pungency: The quality of affecting the sense of smell.

propitious: Kindly disposed.

prosaic: Unimaginative.

proscribe: To reject, as a teaching or a practice, with condemnation or denunciation.

protuberant: Bulging.

provident: Anticipating and making ready for future wants or emergencies.

quiescence: Being quiet, still, or at rest; inactive

quiescent: Being in a state of repose or inaction.

Quixotic: Chivalrous or romantic to a ridiculous or extravagant degree.

quotidian: Of an everyday character; ordinary.

raconteur: A person skilled in telling stories.

pusillanimous: Without spirit or bravery.

pyre: A heap of combustibles arranged for burning a dead body.

qualm: A fit of nausea.

quandary: A puzzling predicament.

quibble: An utterly trivial distinction or objection.

recalcitrant: Marked by stubborn resistance.

recant: To withdraw formally one's belief (in something previously believed or maintained).

reciprocity: Equal mutual rights and benefits granted and enjoyed.

recluse: One who lives in retirement or seclusion.

recondite: Incomprehensible to one of ordinary understanding.

ramify: To divide or subdivide into branches or subdivisions.

rapacious: Seize by force, avaricious

raucous: Harsh.

reactionary: Pertaining to, of the nature of, causing, or favoring reaction.

rebuff: A peremptory or unexpected rejection of advances or approaches.

Describe the following words: recrudescent, recuperate, redoubtable, redress, refractory.

Describe the following words: regale, regicide, reiterate, relapse, remonstrate.

Describe the following words: renovate, repast, repel, repine, reprobate.

Describe the following words: repudiate, repulsive, requisite, requite, rescind.

Describe the following words: resilience, resonance, respite, restive, retinue.

Describe the following words: revere, reverent, ribald, risible, rotund.

regale: To give unusual pleasure.

regicide: The killing of a king or sovereign.

reiterate: To say or do again and again.

relapse: To suffer a return of a disease after partial recovery.

remonstrate: To present a verbal or written protest to those who have power to right or prevent a wrong.

recrudescent: Becoming raw or sore again.

recuperate: To recover.

redoubtable: Formidable.

redress: To set right, as a wrong by compensation or the punishment of the wrong-doer.

refractory: Not amenable to control.

repudiate: To refuse to have anything to do with.

repulsive: Grossly offensive.

requisite: Necessary.

requite: To repay either good or evil to, as to a person.

rescind: To make void, as an act, by the enacting authority or a superior authority.

renovate: To restore after deterioration, as a building.

repast: A meal; figuratively, any refreshment.

repel: To force or keep back in a manner, physically or mentally.

repine: To indulge in fretfulness and faultfinding.

reprobate: One abandoned to depravity and sin.

revere: To regard with worshipful veneration.

reverent: Humble.

ribald: Indulging in or manifesting coarse indecency or obscenity.

risible: Capable of exciting laughter.

rotund: Round from fullness or plumpness.

resilience: The power of springing back to a former position

resonance: Able to reinforce sound by sympathetic vibrations.

respite: Interval of rest.

restive: Resisting control.

retinue: The group of people who accompany an important person during travels.

Describe the following words: ruffian, ruminate, sagacious, salacious, salient.

Describe the following words: salubrious, salutary, sanction, sanguine, sardonic.

Describe the following words: satiate, satyr, savor, scabbard, scintilla.

Describe the following words: scribble, sedulous, sequence, severance, shrewd.

Describe the following words: sinecure, sinuous, skiff, sluggard, solace.

Describe the following words: solvent, somniferous, somnolent, sonorous, sophistry.

salubrious: Healthful; promoting health.

salutary: Beneficial.

sanction: To approve authoritatively.

sanguine: Cheerfully confident; optimistic.

sardonic: Scornfully or bitterly sarcastic.

ruffian: A lawless or recklessly brutal fellow.

ruminate: To chew over again, as food previously swallowed and regurgitated.

sagacious: Able to discern and distinguish with wise perception.

salacious: Having strong sexual desires.

salient: Standing out prominently.

scribble: Hasty, careless writing.

sedulous: Persevering in effort or endeavor.

sequence: The order in which a number or persons, things, or events follow one another in space or time.

severance: Separation.

shrewd: Characterized by skill at understanding and profiting by circumstances.

satiate: To satisfy fully the appetite or desire of.

satyr: A very lascivious person.

savor: To perceive by taste or smell.

scabbard: The sheath of a sword or similar bladed weapon.

scintilla: The faintest ray.

solvent: Having sufficient funds to pay all debts.

somniferous: Tending to produce sleep.

somnolent: Sleepy.

sonorous: Resonant.

sophistry: Reasoning sound in appearance only, especially when designedly deceptive.

sinecure: Any position having emoluments with few or no duties.

sinuous: Curving in and out.

skiff: Usually, a small light boat propelled by oars.

sluggard: A person habitually lazy or idle.

solace: Comfort in grief, trouble, or calamity.

Describe the following words: stanch, stigma, stingy, stolid, submerge.

Describe the following words: soporific, sordid, specious, spurious, squalid.

Describe the following words: supernumerary, supersede, supine, supplicate, suppress.

Describe the following words: subterfuge, succinct, sumptuous, supercilious, superfluous.

Describe the following words: synopsis, taciturn, taut, temerity, terse.

Describe the following words: surcharge, surfeit, susceptibility, sybarite, sycophant.

soporific: Causing sleep; also, something that causes sleep.

sordid: Filthy, morally degraded

specious: Plausible.

spurious: Not genuine.

squalid: Having a dirty, mean, poverty-stricken appearance.

stanch: To stop the flowing of; to check.

stigma: A mark of infamy or token of disgrace attaching to a person as the result of evil-doing.

stingy: Cheap, unwilling to spend money.

stolid: Expressing no power of feeling or perceiving.

submerge: To place or plunge under water.

subterfuge: Evasion.

succinct: Concise.

sumptuous: Rich and costly.

supercilious: Exhibiting haughty and careless contempt.

superfluous: Being more than is needed.

supernumerary: Superfluous.

supersede: To displace.

supine: Lying on the back.

supplicate: To beg.

suppress: To prevent from being disclosed or punished.

surcharge: An additional amount charged.

surfeit: To feed to fullness or to satiety.

susceptibility: A specific capability of feeling or emotion.

sybarite: A luxurious person

sycophant: A servile flatterer, especially of those in authority or influence.

synopsis: A syllabus or summary.

taciturn: Disinclined to conversation.

taut: Stretched tight.

temerity: Foolhardy disregard of danger; recklessness.

terse: Pithy.

Reading Comprehension
© Mometrix Media - flashcardsecrets.com/toefl
TOEFL Essentials

Describe the following words: timorous, torpid, torrid, tortuous, tractable.

Reading Comprehension
© Mometrix Media - flashcardsecrets.com/toefl
TOEFL Essentials

Describe the following words: transgress, transient, transitory, travail, travesty.

Reading Comprehension
© Mometrix Media - flashcardsecrets.com/toefl
TOEFL Essentials

Describe the following words: trenchant, trepidation, trite, truculence, truculent.

Reading Comprehension
© Mometrix Media - flashcardsecrets.com/toefl
TOEFL Essentials

Describe the following words: turbid, turgid, turpitude, tutelage, tyro.

Reading Comprehension
© Mometrix Media - flashcardsecrets.com/toefl
TOEFL Essentials

Describe the following words: ubiquitous, ulterior, umbrage, unctuous, undermine.

Reading Comprehension
© Mometrix Media - flashcardsecrets.com/toefl
TOEFL Essentials

Describe the following words: undulate, untoward, upbraid, vagary, vainglory.

transgress: To break a law.

transient: One who or that which is only of temporary existence.

transitory: Existing for a short time only.

travail: Hard or agonizing labor.

travesty: A grotesque imitation.

timorous: Lacking courage.

torpid: Dull; sluggish; inactive.

torrid: Excessively hot.

tortuous: Abounding in irregular bends or turns.

tractable: Easily led or controlled.

turbid: In a state of turmoil; muddled

turgid: Swollen.

turpitude: Depravity.

tutelage: The act of training or the state of being under instruction.

tyro: One slightly skilled in or acquainted with any trade or profession.

trenchant: Cutting deeply and quickly.

trepidation: Nervous uncertainty of feeling.

trite: Made commonplace by frequent repetition.

truculence: Ferocity.

truculent: Having the character or the spirit of a savage.

undulate: To move like a wave or in waves.

untoward: Causing annoyance or hindrance.

upbraid: To reproach as deserving blame.

vagary: A sudden desire or action

vainglory: Excessive, pretentious, and demonstrative vanity.

ubiquitous: Being present everywhere.

ulterior: Not so pertinent as something else to the matter spoken of.

umbrage: A sense of injury.

unctuous: Oily.

undermine: To subvert in an underhand way.

Reading Comprehension
© Mometrix Media - flashcardsecrets.com/toefl
TOEFL Essentials

Describe the following words: valorous, vapid, variegated, vehement, venal.

Reading Comprehension
© Mometrix Media - flashcardsecrets.com/toefl
TOEFL Essentials

Describe the following words: veneer, venial, veracious, veracity, verbiage.

Reading Comprehension
© Mometrix Media - flashcardsecrets.com/toefl
TOEFL Essentials

Describe the following words: verbose, verdant, veritable, vestige, vicissitude.

Reading Comprehension
© Mometrix Media - flashcardsecrets.com/toefl
TOEFL Essentials

Describe the following words: vigilance, vigilant, virago, virtu, visage.

Reading Comprehension
© Mometrix Media - flashcardsecrets.com/toefl
TOEFL Essentials

Describe the following words: vtiate, vituperate, vivify, vociferous, volatile.

Reading Comprehension
© Mometrix Media - flashcardsecrets.com/toefl
TOEFL Essentials

Describe the following words: voluble, wean, whimsical, winsome, Zeitgeist.

veneer: Outside show or elegance.

venial: That may be pardoned or forgiven, a forgivable sin.

veracious: Habitually disposed to speak the truth.

veracity: Truthfulness.

verbiage: Use of many words without necessity.

valorous: Courageous.

vapid: Having lost sparkling quality and flavor.

variegated: Having marks or patches of different colors; also, varied.

vehement: Very eager or urgent.

venal: Mercenary, corrupt.

vigilance: Alert and intent mental watchfulness in guarding against danger.

vigilant: Being on the alert to discover and ward off danger or insure safety.

virago: Loud talkative women, strong statured women

virtu: Rare, curious, or beautiful quality.

visage: The face, countenance, or look of a person.

verbose: Wordy.

verdant: Green with vegetation.

veritable: Real; true; genuine.

vestige: A visible trace, mark, or impression, of something absent, lost, or gone.

vicissitude: A change, especially a complete change, of condition or circumstances, as of fortune.

voluble: Having great fluency in speaking.

wean: To transfer (the young) from dependence on mother's milk to another form of nourishment.

whimsical: Capricious.

winsome: Attractive.

Zeitgeist: The intellectual and moral tendencies that characterize any age or epoch.

vitiate: To contaminate.

vituperate: To overwhelm with wordy abuse.

vivify: To endue with life.

vociferous: Making a loud outcry.

volatile: Changeable.

Describe the following prefixes: ante, anti, auto, belli, bene.

Describe the following prefixes: A, A, Ab, Ad, Am

Describe the following prefixes: com, contra, cred, de, dem

Describe the following prefixes: bi, bio, cata, chron, circum

Describe the following prefixes: for, fore, homo, hyper, hypo

Describe the following prefixes: dia, dis, epi, equi, ex

A: in, on, of, up, to : abed, afoot

A: without, lacking : atheist, agnostic

Ab: from, away, off : abdicate, abjure

Ad: to, toward : advance

Am: friend, love : amicable, amatory

Ante: before, previous : antecedent, antedate

anti: against, opposing : antipathy, antidote

auto: self : autonomy, autobiography

belli: war, warlike : bellicose

bene: well, good : benefit, benefactor

bi: two : bisect, biennial

bio: life : biology, biosphere

cata: down, away, thoroughly : catastrophe, cataclysm

chron: time : chronometer, synchronize

circum: around : circumspect, circumference

com: with, together, very : commotion, complicate

contra: against, opposing : contradict, contravene

cred: belief, trust : credible, credit

de: from : depart

dem: people : demographics, democracy

dia: through, across, apart : diameter, diagnose

dis: away, off, down, not : dissent, disappear

epi: upon : epilogue

equi: equal, equally : equivalent

ex: out : extract

for: away, off, from : forget, forswear

fore: before, previous : foretell, forefathers

homo: same, equal : homogenized

hyper: excessive, over : hypercritical, hypertension

hypo: under, beneath : hypodermic, hypothesis

Describe the following prefixes: mal, micr, mis, mono, mor

Describe the following prefixes: in, in, inter, intra, magn

Describe the following prefixes: over, pan, para, per, peri

Describe the following prefixes: neo, non, ob, omni, ortho

Describe the following prefixes: pro, re, retro, semi, sub

Describe the following prefixes: phil, poly, post, pre, prim

in: in, into : intrude, invade

in: not, opposing : incapable, ineligible

inter: among, between : intercede, interrupt

intra: within : intramural, intrastate

magn: large : magnitude, magnify

mal: bad, poorly, not : malfunction

micr: small : microbe, microscope

mis: bad, poorly, not : misspell, misfire

mono: one, single : monogamy, monologue

mor: die, death : mortality, mortuary

neo: new : neolithic, neoconservative

non: not : nonentity, nonsense

ob: against, opposing : objection

omni: all, everywhere : omniscient

ortho: right, straight : orthogonal, orthodox

over: above : overbearing

pan: all, entire : panorama, pandemonium

para: beside, beyond : parallel, paradox

per: through : perceive, permit

peri: around : periscope, perimeter

phil: love, like : philosophy, philanthropic

poly: many : polymorphous, polygamous

post: after, following : postpone, postscript

pre: before, previous : prevent, preclude

prim: first, early : primitive, primary

pro: forward, in place of : propel, pronoun

re: back, backward, again : revoke, recur

retro: back, backward : retrospect, retrograde

semi: half, partly : semicircle, semicolon

sub: under, beneath : subjugate, substitute

Describe the following prefixes: uni, vis

Describe the following suffixes: able, age, ance

Describe the following prefixes: super, sym, trans, ultra, un

Describe the following suffixes: dom, en, er, esce, esque

Describe the following suffixes: arch, ard, ate, ation, cy

Describe the following suffixes: ible, ion, ish, ism, ist

Describe the following suffixes: ess, fic, ful, fy, hood

super: above, extra : supersede, supernumerary

sym: with, together : sympathy, symphony

trans: across, beyond, over : transact, transport

ultra: beyond, excessively : ultramodern, ultrasonic, ultraviolet

un: not, reverse of : unhappy, unlock

uni: one : uniform, unity

vis: to see : visage, visible

able: able to, likely : capable, tolerable

age: process, state, rank : passage, bondage

ance: act, condition, fact : acceptance, vigilance

arch: to rule : monarch

ard: one that does excessively : drunkard, wizard

ate: having, showing : separate, desolate

ation: action, state, result : occupation, starvation

cy: state, condition : accuracy, captaincy

dom: state, rank, condition : serfdom, wisdom

en: cause to be, become : deepen, strengthen

er: one who does : teacher

esce: become, grow, continue : convalesce, acquiesce

esque: in the style of, like : picturesque, grotesque

ess: feminine : waitress, lioness

fic: making, causing : terrific, beatific

ful: full of, marked by : thankful, zestful

fy: make, cause, cause to have : glorify, fortify

hood: state, condition : manhood, statehood

ible: able, likely, fit : edible, possible, divisible

ion: action, result, state : union, fusion

ish: suggesting, like : churlish, childish

ism: act, manner, doctrine : barbarism, socialism

ist: doer, believer : monopolist, socialist

Describe the following suffixes: logue, ly, ment, ness, or

Describe the following suffixes: ition, ity, ize, less, like

Describe the following suffixes: ty, ward

Describe the following suffixes: ous, ship, some, th, tude

Fill in your own question.

Fill in your own question.

ition: action, state, result : sedition, expedition

ity: state, quality, condition : acidity, civility

ize: make, cause to be, treat with : sterilize, mechanize, criticize

less: lacking, without : hopeless, countless

like: like, similar : childlike, dreamlike

logue: type of speaking or writing : prologue

ly: like, of the nature of : friendly, positively

ment: means, result, action : refreshment, disappointment

ness: quality, state : greatness, tallness

or: doer, office, action : juror, elevator, honor

ous: marked by, given to : religious, riotous

ship: the art or skill of : statesmanship

some: apt to, showing : tiresome, lonesome

th: act, state, quality : warmth, width

tude: quality, state, result : magnitude, fortitude

ty: quality, state : enmity, activity

ward: in the direction of : backward, homeward

Blank Card

Blank Card